Get Organized Without Losing It

Janet S. Fox

Illustrated by Steve Mark

free spirit
PUBLISHING®

Text copyright © 2017, 2006 by Janet S. Fox
Illustrations copyright © 2017 by Free Spirit Publishing Inc.

Library of Congress Cataloging-in-Publication Data
Names: Fox, Janet S., author.
Title: Get organized without losing it / By Janet S. Fox, illustrated by Steve Mark.
Description: Revised & updated edition. | Minneapolis, MN : Free Spirit Publishing Inc., [2017] | Series: Laugh & learn | Includes index.
Identifiers: LCCN 2017002147 (print) | LCCN 2017006257 (ebook) | ISBN 9781631981739 (pbk.) | ISBN 1631981730 (pbk.) | ISBN 9781631981845 (Web PDF) | ISBN 9781631981852 (ePub)
Subjects: LCSH: Study skills—Handbooks, manuals, etc. | Students—Time management— Handbooks, manuals, etc. | Students—Life skills guides.
Classification: LCC LB1049 .F6 2017 (print) | LCC LB1049 (ebook) | DDC 371.3/0281—dc23
LC record available at https://lccn.loc.gov/2017002147

Reading Level Grade 4; Interest Level Ages 8–13;
Fountas & Pinnell Guided Reading Level S

Edited by Pamela Espeland and Eric Braun
Cover and interior design by Emily Dyer
Illustrations by Steve Mark

Additional graphics: clipboard p. 35 © Angela Jones | Dreamstime.com; planner pp. 40–41, 91 © Gmm2000 | Dreamstime.com; chess piece pp. 80, 84–85, © Cory Thoman | Dreamstime.com

10 9 8 7 6 5 4 3 2 1
Printed in the United States of America
V20300617

Free Spirit Publishing Inc.
6325 Sandburg Road, Suite 100
Minneapolis, MN 55427–3674
(612) 338-2068
help4kids@freespirit.com
www.freespirit.com

FSC
www.fsc.org
MIX
Paper from
responsible sources
FSC® C005010

Dedication

For Jeff and Kevin: With you by my side,
I'm never lost.

And for Barbara, my mom, who also
loved words.

Acknowledgments

Special thanks to Kathy Whitehead and
Shirley Hoskins; to Jane Beatty; to Kiri
Jorgensen; to Dudley, BJ, and June; and to
my students and colleagues at St. Michael's.
Your guidance and support are invaluable.

My thanks to Larry Rand, who taught
me in ninth grade how to get organized.

Thank you to my editors, Trina Wentzel,
Eric Braun, and the exceptional Pamela
Espeland. To Steve Mark for his wonderful
illustrations. And to Judy Galbraith,
Marjorie Lisovskis, and all at Free Spirit who
recognize that kids need loving guidance.

Contents

Is It Time to Get Organized?

Take this quick quiz to find out.

QUICK QUIZ

2. Do you spend tons of time looking for things you need in order to do your schoolwork or homework?

9. Do you feel like you're always running behind?

1. Is your desk at school a disaster?

6. Is your school locker a shocker?

7. Is your backpack a `black hole`*?

4. Would your head fall off if it weren't fastened on?

10. Have you ever missed out on fun because your schoolwork didn't get done?

5. Are you forever losing the stuff you need in order to do your schoolwork or homework?

3. Do you wish you were more organized?

8. Are the questions on this quiz numbered in the right order?

*** Black hole:** A place in space where everything gets sucked in and disappears.

If you answered **YES** to one or more of the questions on the quiz, keep reading. Help is on the way.

If you answered **NO** to question #8, terrific! You can tell when things are organized—and when they're not.

Hey, that's a start.

Picture This

You plop down in your seat at school seconds before the bell rings. The teacher announces a pop quiz, and you search high and low for a pencil. When you finally find one, it needs sharpening, but there's no time.

During the quiz, you change your mind about the answer to question #3. But the eraser on your pencil is flat, and you rub a big black smudge on the paper. You waste time trying to fix it. When the teacher calls "Time's up!" you're still not finished with the quiz.

Then the teacher asks for yesterday's homework. You dig through your backpack, which is crammed with crumpled papers—everything but your homework.

Is it still on the kitchen table at home? Or maybe under your bed? You can't remember, and it's too late anyway. No homework means another zero.

When you get home after soccer, you watch TV for a while. Then you eat dinner, help with the dishes, and play with the dog.

About an hour before bedtime, you go into your room and dump the contents of your backpack on the floor. You realize you forgot your science book. Oh, no! There's a test tomorrow! At least you've got your class notes . . .

You reach for your binder, which is so overstuffed that it pops open and papers fly everywhere. Your science notes—when you finally find them—are illegible, and what you can read makes no sense.

You try to study for the test, but what's the use? You give up and mess around on your phone instead. When you finally go to bed, you are way too worried to sleep.

The bad news is—you probably won't do well on the test. The good news is—things don't have to be this way.

By the time the next test comes around, you can be a new person. Someone who's calm. Someone who's organized. Someone who's ready to do your best work.

TIP: Being organized does **not** mean being a total neat freak. It means spending **less** time going crazy and **more** time having fun.

Chapter 1

Basic Tools for Getting Organized

To get organized, you don't need fancy furniture or a smartphone loaded with apps. You don't need special computer software or a tablet with built-in calendars.

You don't even need a parent who says, "Do your homework!" "What died in your backpack?" or "You're going to miss the bus AGAIN!"

What you **do** need are some basic tools. Let's start with things that will get you **to and from** school.

A sturdy backpack with proper straps, made of durable material, and having at least two compartments. Keep your everyday going-to-school stuff—house keys, wallet, calculator, folding umbrella—in the smaller compartment(s). Use the larger one(s) for your binder, folders, laptop or tablet, and books.

Some schools have rules about backpacks. Like: No solid backpacks—mesh or see-through only. No rolling backpacks—they can be a tripping hazard. (Rolling backpacks lighten the load for many kids, but some schools still won't allow them. Or they allow them but make kids carry them inside the school building . . . which kind of misses the whole point.) To make sure you don't get the wrong kind of backpack, ask your teacher or check on your school website before you buy.

THE CURSE OF THE TOO-HEAVY BACKPACK

Does your backpack weigh almost as much as you do? Thousands of kids are injured each year because of overloaded backpacks. Experts say that your backpack should weigh no more than 10 percent of your weight. In other words, if you weigh 90 pounds, your backpack should weigh 9 pounds. Not empty . . . `full`.

Some kids carry backpacks that weigh as much as 45 pounds! No wonder they have back pain, neck pain, or shoulder pain. Sometimes this causes kids to miss out on school or sports activities.

So travel as light as you can. Carry only what you really need. Don't load up on personal items. Don't carry your NASA shuttlecraft model to school (for a whole lot of reasons). And even if it looks cool to sling your backpack over one shoulder, don't. Wear it like it's made to be worn: on your back, using both straps.

Adjust the straps so the weight of the backpack hangs in the middle of your back, where your muscles are strongest. If your backpack has a waist strap, use it. And, by the way, a light plastic sack with string straps is not a backpack. If you carry one of those you could end up with sore shoulders and crumpled papers.

TIP: For many kids, the heaviest things in their backpacks are their textbooks. If lugging textbooks to and from home is a problem for you, start by bringing home only the books you need for that night's homework (or that weekend's study). No science assignment? Leave the science textbook in your locker.

Some schools keep a classroom set for use in school, so you can keep your set at home. Other schools use digital textbooks that you can access on your computer or tablet.

If you're still loaded down with textbooks, talk with your teacher.

One or more homework folders. A homework folder is any folder with two pockets. The pocket on the **left** is for homework you need to do. Label it "Home." The pocket on the **right** is for homework you've done. Label it "School." You may need a homework folder for each subject, so check with your teachers.

You can make a homework folder using heavy paper and tape or staples.

A really good binder. The best ones have a locking ring mechanism—the kind that snaps open and closed. If (make that **when**) you drop your binder, everything won't fall out. Otherwise, that's a surefire way to ruin your day.

What **size** binder is best? One with 1½" or 2" rings. That should be enough to hold five school subjects.

Some binders have a clear plastic cover sleeve. You might use it to hold an assignment sheet, your class schedule, or your homework checklist (more about that later).

MY SCHEDULE

Period	Class	Room #
1	Math	212
2	ELA	235
3	Fitness	Gym
4	Hip Hop Dancing	115
	Lunch	Cafeteria
5	History	121
6	Earth Science	252

Some schools have rules about binders. Like: No giant three-ring binders. They're too big to fit in many desks and too heavy to carry unless you're an Olympic weightlifter.

Things to keep your binder organized. Like:

- **Subject dividers.** Colorful subject dividers make it easier to find things in your binder. Be sure to label the tabs by subject: English, Science, History, Math, Geography. You can even divide subjects into sections. In English, you might want separate tabs for Vocabulary, Spelling, and Writing.

TIP: You might add a Personal Reference Section tab up front. Keep commonly misspelled words, math facts, science facts, how-to lists, and other helpful study tools there.

- **A supply of blank paper.** Make sure you keep a good supply of blank paper in your binder for note-taking or pop quizzes. (But, um, not for passing notes to classmates.)

- **A zippered pencil pouch.** Your pouch should be big enough to hold two to three sharpened pencils, an eraser, and a short ruler. It should have a pre-punched edge that fits the rings of your binder.

- **Sheet protectors.** These clear plastic sleeves protect important handouts and other papers from smudges, spills, and tears. If your teacher gives you a handout listing all of the math assignments for the year, put it in a sheet protector. If you spend hours coloring in the countries on a map of the world, put it in a sheet protector. You can keep these at home or in your locker until you need them.

- **Two-pocket, three-hole-punched folders.** Sometimes you have a stack of handouts you need to keep together. These folders do the job. Like subject dividers, they come in colors.

TIP: To be super-organized, you can color-coordinate your folders with your subject dividers.

You also need some basic tools to keep it together **in** school. You can stash these tools in your desk or locker:

A small box to hold pencils, erasers, and other small items. Many stores sell standard plastic school-supply boxes.

You can decorate a small cardboard box you find at home, like a shoebox, but check first that it fits in your desk or locker and holds everything you need.

Things to go in the box. These are the school supplies that most students need. Check with your teacher to find out if you should have anything else.

- 4 or 5 sharpened pencils with good erasers

- rubber eraser

- small pencil sharpener

- scissors

- small ruler

- small bottle of glue or glue stick

- roll of clear adhesive tape

- paper clips

- small stapler

- highlighters

- colored pencils

- a portable 3-hole punch

Make a copy of the shopping list on pages 20–21, or download the list at freespirit.com/organize. Check off the things you already have. The extra lines are for writing other things you may need. (There are a few things on this list we haven't talked about yet, but be patient—we will.)

Show the list to a parent or other family grown-up and ask for help getting your supplies. Bring the list to your local discount store or office supplies store. Many grocery and drug stores also sell these items.

If you can't get everything at once, work your way down the list.

My Get-Organized Shopping List

- ☐ Backpack with at least two compartments
- ☐ Homework folder
- ☐ 1½" to 2" three-ring binder, with a locking ring if possible
- ☐ Supply of blank lined note paper
- ☐ Subject dividers
- ☐ Zippered pencil pouch
- ☐ Sheet protectors

- ☐ Scissors
- ☐ Small ruler
- ☐ Small bottle of glue or glue stick
- ☐ Roll of clear adhesive tape
- ☐ Paper clips
- ☐ Small stapler
- ☐ Highlighters
- ☐ Colored pencils
- ☐ Portable three-hole punch

- [ ] Two-pocket, three-hole-punched folders

- [ ] Small supply box for desk or locker items

- [ ] About 10 sharpened pencils (some for your pencil pouch, some for your supply box)

- [ ] Two rubber erasers (one for your pouch, one for your box)

- [ ] Two small pencil sharpeners (one for your pouch, one for your box)

- [ ] Locker shelves

- [ ] Magnetic locker hooks

- [ ] Magnetic locker file pockets

- [ ] Plastic stacking drawers for your locker

- [ ] Student planner

- [ ] _____

- [ ] _____

- [ ] _____

- [ ] _____

Chapter 2

Desk Disasters, Locker Shockers, and Other Major Messes

Which of these statements is true for you?

1. My desk and locker at school are neat and tidy. There's a place for everything. I can always find what I need.

2. My desk and locker are kind of messy. I can usually find what I need, but it might take a while.

3. My desk is a disaster and my locker is a shocker.

If you picked #1, you can probably skip this part of the book. Take a bike ride, listen to music, read a book, call a friend, or go invent something.

Did you pick #2 or #3? Stay put and keep reading.

How to Survive a Desk Disaster

Your desk is not a wastebasket. It's easy to toss that used tissue into your desk (ewww!), but it's better to toss it into the trash.

Your desk is not a homework folder. Stuff homework into your desk and you might as well feed it to the dog. Use your homework folder instead.

Your desk is not a refrigerator. Don't use your desk to store food, which you'll probably forget about until it rots and smells horrible and grows mold.

Let's start with a **cleanup**. Go through your desk as soon as you can. Toss the trash. Put important papers where they belong—in your binder or your homework folder.

Some teachers allow time for a weekly classroom cleanup. If that doesn't happen in your classroom, plan to take a few minutes on your own. Friday at the end of the school day is a good time to tackle this task. That way, when you return to school on Monday morning, you'll find a nice, clean desk waiting for you.

Try not to fall over from the surprise.

Q: Some people say that a messy desk is a sign of a **creative** mind. Others say that a messy desk is a sign of a **cluttered** mind. Still others say that a clean desk means you're a neat freak. Who's right and who's wrong?

A: Who cares? What matters is what works for you. But for most people, a messy desk is a big time-waster.

How to Handle a Locker Shocker

NEWS FLASH! . . . Student Opens Locker Door, Is Crushed To Death By Falling Objects . . . . . .

NEWS BULLETIN! . . . Student Opens Locker Door, Faints From Awful Stink Of Ancient Gym Clothes . . . . .

NEWS CRAWL! . . . Student Spends Years Searching Locker For Permission Slip, Misses Field Trip, Doesn't Graduate . . . .

Get the message? Similar to your desk, your locker is not a wastebasket, a homework folder, or a refrigerator. Plus, it's not a dirty clothes bin, a dumpster, or one of those self-storage places people rent to hold all the stuff that won't fit in their closet or garage.

Your locker is where you put your coat or jacket, books, supplies, gym clothes, lunchbox, and other items while you're in class. It's where you store stuff you'll need to find during the school day.

Some schools have rules about kids carrying backpacks during the school day. It's okay to carry your backpack to and from school, but once you arrive at school, away it goes—in your locker.

Let's start with a locker cleanup. Get rid of anything that doesn't belong. Not sure if that hard, shriveled orange stick is a crayon or a carrot from last month's lunch? When in doubt, throw it out.

Do you need extra help organizing what does belong in your locker? Many students find these locker tools useful:

- locker shelves
- magnetic hooks
- magnetic file pockets
- plastic stacking drawers

These tools are included on the shopping list on pages 20–21.

Some schools have rules about some locker tools. Check first to find out what's allowed at your school.

Pssst!

Sometimes a messy desk or locker doesn't mean you're a slob. It means there are other things going on in your life, and you just can't handle being organized right now.

Maybe you're having trouble paying attention or listening in school. Maybe you don't understand the directions the teacher gives you. Maybe you can't see the board or you can't read the teacher's handwriting.

Maybe you're so far behind with your schoolwork that you think you'll never catch up. Maybe school is so boring for you that you just don't care. Or maybe things are happening at home that make it hard for you to focus at school.

TIP: If a messy desk or locker is the least of your worries, talk to an adult you trust. Start with a parent, another family grown-up, or a teacher you like. If your school has a counselor and/or nurse, talk with him or her. School counselors and school nurses are good listeners.

How to Manage Other Major Messes

Once you've tackled your desk and your locker, cleaning out your backpack and binder will be a breeze.

Best of all, you can do this at home. You don't have to organize your personal things at school, where time is crunched and your teachers and classmates are nearby. No one needs to see all those gross things you find!

Start with your backpack—the place most likely to be a biohazard.*

*Biohazard: Something that is very bad for you and the environment. Like a year-old tuna sandwich.

1. Clear your room of curious family pets and small children. (It's for their own safety.)

2. After you've emptied your backpack of books, notebooks, folders, and electronic devices, turn it upside-down and dump the rest of its contents on the floor. Shake it to make sure even the stickiest, most stubborn items fall out.

3. Sort the debris. Go through loose papers and put them where they belong—in your handy homework folder, or your binder, or the recycling bin. Sharpen loose pencils and put them back in your pencil pouch. Put gross, smelly clothes in the laundry and put garbage where it belongs.

4. If anything in the debris pile tries to crawl away, hit it with your shoe or save it for a science project.

Backpack neat and tidy? Move on to your binder. No problem—you're an expert who knows the routine. Sort, recycle what you don't need, and put the rest of your papers where they belong.

Give yourself a high-five when you're done. You've accomplished a lot. Nothing will ever be this hard again—unless you slide back into your old ways. Which you won't, if you follow the checkup habit.

Give Yourself Regular Checkups

Open wide and say aaahhhhh.

1. Each day, before you start your homework, take everything out of your backpack. Sort, trash, recycle, and put things where they belong.

2. Each week, clean out your desk and locker.

3. Every week or two, check your in-school supply box. Take it home and ask a parent or other family adult to help you replenish your supplies.

4. Every couple of weeks, go through your binder. Recycle anything you know you don't need or want anymore. But keep older handouts, quizzes, and tests safely at home, in case you need them to study for a test later in the semester. If you're not sure what to do with some of your papers, ask a parent or other family adult for advice.

Chapter 3

Plan for School Success

You've cleaned out your desk, your locker, your backpack, and your binder.* Everything is where it belongs. You can find what you need when you need it.

You're ready to make a plan for school success. For this, you'll need a few new tools and strategies.

*You **have** cleaned them out, right?

MONDAY
Wake up
Wake up my people
Eat
Walk
Nap
Get treats
Check for Squirrels
Nap
Eat
Walk
Bedtime

TUESDAY Repeat Monday

WEDNESDAY Repeat Tuesday

THURSDAY Repeat Wednesday

F

Use a Student Planner

To make a plan, you need (duh) a planner.

There are about a zillion different student planners to choose from. Visit an office supply store and look around. Or go online, search for "student planners," and click on a few links.

Some websites have planner templates (forms) you can download, print out, and start using right away. Ask your teacher or media specialist for help finding these. You can even create your own forms.

There are many different types of student planners.

Monthly view planners show a whole month on two pages. (Not much writing room there.)

Weekly view planners show one week on two pages. This is the size that most students use.

Two-page-per-day planners are great if you also like to use your planner as a journal or daily diary.

Some planners just have the days and dates, with blank lines or spaces for writing. Some look more like assignment notebooks, with subject names and boxes to check when you finish each assignment.

Some planners have places to write lists of things to take home and bring to school, weekly goals, long-term projects, teacher and parent messages, and more.

Electronic calendars that come as an app on your phone have many advantages. You can program the app to give you alerts for events—like that history test or your class field trip. You can print out the calendar to have a hard copy when it syncs with your home computer, which is useful for long-term planning (which we'll talk about in a minute). You can even coordinate events with your family's calendar, so you won't forget about dinner with Grandma. One disadvantage with a calendar app is that some schools don't allow you to use your phone or tablet in class, so check the school website to know the rules.

Some schools provide students with planners. Often, these have the school logo on the cover and a special section with school handbook pages, schedules, and maps. Or your school might provide an electronic planner to use on a tablet or other device. If your school provides a planner, that's the one you should use.

9 Great Reasons to Use a Student Planner

1. **A planner is portable.** You can carry yours to and from school in your backpack.

2. **A planner never forgets.** Unlike the human head, it has no holes in it, so things can't fall out.

3. **A planner prevents scheduling problems.** Did a friend invite you to go skating two Saturdays from now? Check your planner before saying yes. Uh-oh, that's the day of the track meet and the day before that big history test!

4. **A planner keeps all of your important information in one place.** No more paper scraps, sticky notes, or inky, smeared reminders written on your hand.

5. **A planner reminds you of what you need to do and when.** You will no longer need parents, teachers, or other adults in your life. (Just kidding.)

6. **A planner helps you keep track of important projects.** Write down everything you need to do, and you're less likely to forget a task or a due date.

7. **A planner helps you reach your goals.** Break down a big goal into smaller steps (you'll learn more about this in a minute): Write each step in your planner, and finish one step at a time. Before you know it, you're there.

8. **A planner can be whatever you want it to be.** Yours might be a simple list of homework assignments, school projects, and activities. Or it might include your address book, lists of books you want to read and movies you want to see, your daily journal, notes about ideas you have, your hopes and dreams. . . . What else? It's up to you.

9. **A planner frees up valuable space in your brain.** When you write down many things you need to remember, you don't actually need to remember them. You just need to remember **one** thing: to look in your planner.

Try these planner tips and tricks:

- If you're extra busy with homework and activities, use a `daily planner`. If you're not so busy, use a **weekly planner**.

- When you first get your planner, spend time checking it out. Decide how you'll use it. Where will you write long-term assignments? After-school activities? How will you keep track of your goals so you're sure to reach them? **Personalize** your planner. Make it your own.

- Write in your planner in **pencil**, not ink. That way, when things change, you can erase them instead of crossing them out.

- Mark really important events and due dates with a `highlighter` or `stick-on stars`.

- Use different colored **highlighters** or **colored pencils** for different subjects or types of activities.

- If you have an electronic planner or calendar, use the alert function. You can tell your planner to remind you ahead of time when things are due or when you have events like sports practice or (ugh) dentist appointments. That way you don't miss them.

- Remember that all work and no play makes life dull, dull, dull . . . zzzzzzzzzzz. Be sure to leave room for fun times, relaxing times, and special times with friends and family. Write those in your planner, too.

- Check your planner **first thing every morning**. You'll know what the day will bring.

- Check your planner **last thing every night**. You'll go to sleep feeling ready for tomorrow.

Plan to Manage Your Time

A planner helps you see what's happening in your life. Let's look now at how to prevent event overload.

Your time at school is already organized. School starts and ends at the same time each day. Lunch happens at the same time. You know when you'll be in science, in math, and in homeroom.

Some of your time outside of school is probably organized, too. You may have sports, scouts, music lessons, and other places you have to be during the week.

Are you a good time manager? Do you spend your time wisely or waste it? You'll probably waste a lot **less** time now that you've cleaned out your desk, locker, backpack, and binder, because you won't be searching high and low for your stuff.＊ You need to manage your **time** just as well as you're now managing your space.

＊It would also help if you cleaned your **room**, but that's a topic for another book.

On a sheet of lined paper, make a list of the things you usually do after school on a normal weekday. Your list might look something like this:

Activity	Estimated Time	Actual Time
Go to swim team practice		
Chill out at home		
Have a snack		
Watch TV		
Play a video game		
Text with friends		
Set the table for dinner		
Eat dinner		
Help clean up after dinner		
Watch TV		
Do homework		
Play on the computer		
Get ready for bed		

Once you've made your list, **estimate** how much time you spend on each thing. Write your estimates on your list.

Activity	Estimated Time	Actual Time
Go to swim team practice	45 minutes	
Chill out at home	10 minutes	
Have a snack	5 minutes	
Watch TV	20 minutes	
Play a video game	10 minutes	
Text with friends	15 minutes	
Set the table for dinner	5 minutes	
Eat dinner	20 minutes	
Help clean up after dinner	20 minutes	
Watch TV	30 minutes	
Do homework	60 minutes	
Play on the computer	10 minutes	
Get ready for bed	10 minutes	

The next school day, record the real times you spend on each thing. Compare the real times with the estimates.

What do you see?

That you spend more time texting than you thought? That you play video games for two hours but do homework for only 10 minutes?

How could you make better use of your time? You'll need a parent or other family adult to help you figure out the answer to this question.

Make a copy of the After-School Scheduler on pages 50–51 or download one from freespirit.com/organize. Sit down with your parent or other adult and fill in your chores, responsibilities, and activities for a typical week. These are blocks of time that don't change. Lightly color in these blocks with a colored pencil.

Time	Monday	Tuesday	Wednesday	Thursday	Friday
2:30–3:00	Travel to home, after-school activities				
3:00–3:30	Piano lessons	Volleyball practice		Volleyball practice	
3:30–4:00	Travel				

The blank places on the chart show how much time you have for homework and studying, plus your free time. Now you can plan your homework and study time first and then your free time. *

*Not the other way around.

After-School Scheduler

Time	Monday	Tuesday	Wednesday	Thursday	Friday
2:30–3:00					
3:00–3:30					
3:30–4:00					
4:00–4:30					
4:30–5:00					
5:00–5:30					

5:30–6:00						
6:00–6:30						
6:30–7:00						
7:00–7:30						
7:30–8:00						
8:00–8:30						
8:30–9:00						

Plan for Homework

Now that you can see your homework and study time, here's how to make the most of it.

Use a homework checklist. See pages 54–55 for a homework checklist you can copy or download from freespirit.com/organize. Staple or clip it to the front of your homework folder, or slip it into the clear plastic sleeve of your binder. Start each week with a fresh copy.

Leave your homework folder on top of your desk. Use the checklist to remind you what you need to take home that day in order to do your homework. Ask your teacher to double-check your list at the end of the day for a few days until you feel comfortable with the routine.

Have a regular homework time. Some kids do their homework right after school. Other kids run off steam first and then do their homework. What works best for you?

Talk it over with your parents or other family adults. Then decide on a regular homework time—a set time when you'll do your homework every day. On some days, you may have to adjust due to other appointments or commitments, but it works best if you stick close to the same time each day.

TIP: Even when you don't have homework, use your homework time to learn. Read a book, study your math facts or spelling words, or work on a long-term project.

Homework Checklist

Things I need to take home with me	Monday	Tuesday	Wednesday	Thursday	Friday
Planner					
Filled out					
Checked by teacher					
Textbooks					
Workbooks					
Worksheets/ handouts					
Notebooks					

		Special notes, permissions, forms to be signed by parent/caregiver			
		_____ (What else?)			
		_____ (What else?)			
		_____ (What else?)			

Q: How much time each day should I spend on homework?

A: About 10 minutes per grade. So, if you're in third grade, you should spend about 30 minutes each day on homework. In fourth grade, about 40 minutes. In sixth grade, about an hour. If you're in grade 730, plan to spend 7,300 minutes every day doing homework.

But seriously: If you regularly spend hours and hours and hours doing homework, ask a parent or other family adult to talk with your teacher. Life is more than homework.

Have a regular homework place. One day you do your homework at the kitchen table, the next on the living room floor, the day after in the bathtub while singing along with your favorite band . . .

Sorry, that won't cut it. If possible, you should do your homework in the same place every day. Someplace quiet where you can work without being bothered or distracted.

If you have your own room and your own desk or table there, great. If not, ask a parent or other family grown-up to help you find a regular quiet study space, like a table in the corner of the family room. If you work in a family space, like in the kitchen or at the dining room table, you'll want a box or two to hold your supplies, so you can quickly put things away when your homework is done and the family needs that space.

These are the things you might want in your homework space, wherever it is:

- **A comfortable chair that supports your lower back.** It's fine to read a story sprawled on a sofa or beanbag chair, but for homework, you should sit up fairly straight. Your chair should also be the right height so you can keep both feet on the floor and work without hunching over.

- **A strong light.** A bright light overhead is good. A desk lamp over your shoulder is better.

- **Study supplies** like the ones you keep at school (paper, pencils, sharpener, eraser, scissors, ruler, glue, tape, paper clips, stapler, staples, highlighters, colored pencils) and a few more (calculator, three-hole punch, markers). Store these in a plastic box so you can put them out of the way when you're finished working, especially if you're working in a family space.

- **A computer with Internet access** so you can use online reference tools like dictionaries and maps, access the school website, and get other materials from teachers. Many schools put assignments, due dates, readings, handouts, and so on online. Some schools provide students with a tablet or laptop. If you don't have access

to a computer or the Internet at home, talk to your teacher. Public libraries provide patrons with computers and Internet access, too.

- **A big plastic file box, large binder, or stacking plastic drawers.** Store class notes, handouts, old quizzes, and other papers you don't need at the moment. At the end of the school year, you'll have a history of what you did and a handy reference for any final tests.

Q: Which homework assignments should I do first? The easiest or the hardest?

A: That depends. Sometimes it's nice to get the easy things out of the way first (the spelling list, the math worksheet) and then tackle the tough ones (the history project). Sometimes doing a hard assignment first makes everything else seem like a piece of cake. You can decide each day how you feel. Number each assignment in your planner in the order in which you'll do it.

Use a task timeline. A task timeline breaks any assignment into smaller pieces—and puts you in control of your time. It helps you pace yourself so you don't rush through an assignment or take all night to do it.

A task timeline might look like this:

Write a Paragraph About Cats		
Planning →	Working →	Checking
5 minutes	10 minutes	5 minutes

A *chorus* line might look like this:

You don't need a chorus line. You need a timeline.

Your timeline shows that you'll spend 5 minutes organizing your ideas for the paragraph (planning), 10 minutes writing (working), and 5 minutes correcting and proofreading (checking).

For a math assignment, you could use your planning time to estimate the answers to math problems.

Deal with Distractions

These days, it seems, most kids **multitask**. They talk on phones, play games on the phone, text their friends, use social media, watch TV, and listen to tunes while studying the words for tomorrow's spelling test.

Hey, if they can do this and still do well in school, good for them.

Not everyone can study and learn with distractions. In fact, most kids do much better with **quiet**. If that includes you, try these tips.

- Turn off the TV, videos, music, smartphone, and computer (unless you're using it for research). Turn off your notifications. Now it's just you and your homework. Guess you'd better get it done.

- Ask your siblings not to bug you while you're doing your homework. If they bug you anyway, go to a parent or other family grown-up for help.

- Make a "Do Not Disturb" sign to hang on your door—or to put on the kitchen table, if that's your regular homework spot.

- When random thoughts invade your brain ("I wonder if he/she likes me . . . What was that mystery meat I had for lunch today?"), don't try to block them. Instead, write them down on a note pad or scrap paper. Then set it aside.

- If your homework place is noisy, try listening to soft music through headphones. Instrumental music (music without words) is less distracting.

If you've tried everything and you still can't study, maybe you're tired, hungry, or bored. Take a short nap, eat a healthy snack, or shoot some hoops. The homework will still be there when you return.

Homework is like that—it won't go away.

Chapter 4

Plan to Be Ready for School Each Day

Is your morning a **blur** of getting dressed, gulping breakfast, and dashing out the door?

Do you often **forget** things you're supposed to bring to school?

Are you already stressed out by the time you get to school?

That's no way to start your day. So don't. Here are some tips to make the start of your school day go more smoothly.

You forgot something!

Get Off to a Good Start

Pick out your clothes the night before. The five minutes before you rush to catch the bus or carpool is not the time to decide if the striped shirt goes with the plaid pants. (Hint: It probably doesn't.) Hang your clothes front and center in your closet or drape them over a chair in your room. And try not to change your mind in the morning.

If you wear a school uniform, you're lucky. Even if you think it's dorky. A school uniform means one less decision you have to make at night before you go to bed.

Pack your lunch the night before. If it's your job to pack your own lunch for school, do it before you go to bed at night. You might have the kitchen all to yourself and get first dibs on the best apple.

Try to pack a healthy lunch. You'll have more energy for the afternoon. Avoid fried snacks, cookies, candy, white bread, and soda. Give trail mix, air-popped popcorn, turkey on whole-grain bread, real fruit, and water a chance. If you're in the habit of packing junky lunches, ask a parent or other family adult to help you do a meal makeover.

TIP: If you don't bring your lunch to school, be sure to put tomorrow's lunch money or lunch voucher where you won't forget it. Put it in your shoe or in the small compartment of your backpack.

Is That Your Lunch Box or a Garbage Can?

What's that mushy brown thing? Must be last week's half-eaten banana. And the carton with the slimy stuff at the bottom? Looks like it once was blueberry yogurt. The moldy, mysterious slab? Could be an ancient sandwich.

Would you eat out of a garbage can? Probably not. So don't treat your lunch box like one. Bring it home from school every night and clean it out. Throw away perishables. Put the uneaten orange back in the fridge. Wash reusable containers in hot, soapy water. Then wash and dry your lunch box, too. You'll have a clean, fresh place to put tomorrow's yummy lunch.

Plan your breakfast the night before. It's a fact: Kids who eat breakfast do better in school. So don't skip breakfast—and don't just stuff your face with sugary cereal or toaster waffles swimming in sticky syrup. Try some whole-grain toast or cereal, an egg, fruit, and a glass of milk or orange juice.

Pile everything you need next to the door you use when you leave for school. Put your coat, hat, boots, backpack, binder, tablet, gloves, school project, and gym clothes—anything you don't want to forget the next day—right where you'll be sure to see them.

TIP: When you make time each night to get ready for school, you start the next day feeling calm and in control. You're more relaxed when you get to school because you know you have everything you need.

Plan for Long-Term Projects

Many students dread long-term projects. But their parents dread them even more.

Kid: Mom, can you take me to the library tonight?

Mom: The library is closed tonight. Why?

Kid: I have a history project.

Mom: What kind of history project?

Kid: A report on the Civil War. We're supposed to read a book and write a paper and draw a map and build a three-dimensional battlefield model and make a soldier's costume.

Mom: All that? Wow. And when is this project due?

Kid: Tomorrow. Can you help?

Life is easier for you and your parents when you get long-term projects done on time. Here's how.

1. Start early. Don't wait until the last minute.

2. Write the project due date in your student planner. Write it in red, or circle it in red, or draw flowers or stars or arrows around it—anything that makes it stand out.

3. Make a list of all the things you need to do for the project. Don't worry about the order at first. Just list everything. You're breaking down the project into baby steps—the trick to getting it done. (The treat comes later: *being* done.)

4. Decide what steps you'll do first, second, and so on. Number your list.

5. Make a copy of the Long-Term Project Planner on pages 76–77 or download a copy from freespirit.com/organize. Write down the steps you need to complete and when you need to complete them. Use the spaces on the calendar part of the Project Planner to describe what you will do each day—your tasks for that day. You'll find an example of a filled-in Project Planner on pages 78–79.

6. Write each day's tasks in your student planner. Then you can see how and where they fit in with your other responsibilities.

7. Figure out how much time you'll need to do each task. Write the times in your student planner. **Example:** You estimate that it will take you two hours to search the library for books you need. You add that time to your homework schedule for Tuesday and Wednesday.

8. Stick to your plan. If you miss a day, get back to work the next day.

9. See step #1.

TIP: Always give yourself more time than you think you'll really need. That way, when you finish early, you'll have plenty of time to celebrate—or relax.

Don't procrastinate! Focus on each baby step toward your goal. Take little breaks between steps. Keep doing the steps and your project will get done.

The first time or two you plan a long-term project, it might seem like a lot to sort out. Ask an adult for help. Any parent or family adult who has ever been stuck with a last-minute project will be glad to help you plan. Any teacher who has ever heard long, boring excuses about why a project isn't done will be happy to help.

You won't believe what happened. There was a bright light outside my window, then a noise like a giant vacuum cleaner, and this big homework-sucking spaceship attached a hose to my window and then...

Long-Term Project Planner _____

Assignment: _____

    Additions: _____

    Additions: _____

How long will assignment take to complete? _____days

Steps to complete:	By when:
1.	
2.	
3.	
4.	
5.	
6.	

	Monday	Tuesday	Wednesday	
Week 1				
Week 2				
Week 3				

Date assigned: _____ Due date: _____

Number of days until due: _____

Notes:

	Thursday	**Friday**	Saturday	Sunday

Long-Term Project Planner (Example)

Assignment: <u>Report on Civil War</u>

    Additions: <u>Maps, diagrams, pictures</u>

    Additions: <u>Costume</u>

How long will assignment take to complete? <u> 17 </u> days

Steps to complete:	By when:
1. find books	October 5
2. take notes	October 9
3. make outline	October 11
4. write report	October 17
5. find maps, etc.	October 18
6. make costume	October 20

	Monday	Tuesday	Wednesday	
Week 1	10/3 Get assignment	10/4 Search library and online	10/5 Search library	
Week 2	10/10 Start outline	10/11 Finish outline	10/12 Write; work on costume	
Week 3	10/17 Finish final draft	10/18 Finish maps	10/19 Work on costume	

Date assigned: **October 3**   Due date: **October 21**

Number of days until due: **18**

Notes:

the library closes early on Fridays

	Thursday	Friday	Saturday	Sunday
	10/6 Take notes; start costume	10/7 Take notes	10/8 Take notes	10/9 Finish notes
	10/13 Write	10/14 Finish rough draft	10/15 Write final draft	10/16 Work on maps, etc.
	10/20 Finish costume	10/21 Hand in report	Celebrate!	

Plan to Learn

Now you have the plan and the time—but do you have the **information** you need? A few simple strategies can help you organize your thoughts.

Simple Strategy 1
Take Good Class Notes

For this, you'll need special note-taking paper. All it will cost is a little time—because you'll make it yourself using your regular lined paper, a ruler, and a red pencil.

About two inches from the left-hand side of the page, draw a **vertical** (up-and-down) **red line** down the whole length of the page. Do this on 10 pages (or more) and put them in the front of your binder.

When you are listening to your teacher, use the wider **right-hand column** to write notes in short sentences. (Don't worry about grammar and punctuation. These notes are just for you.)

Use the narrower **left-hand column** to write key words—the most important words your teacher says. For example, list names of people and places, dates, and big ideas.

Middle Ages	From 5th century to 15th century
Visigoths	Germans who invaded Rome
Feudalism	Serfs worked on land but didn't own it

If your teacher says something like, "This is important," "Remember this," or especially (hello!) "This will be on the test," mark that note with a star.

If your teacher **writes** something on the board, add it to your notes.

If your teacher **repeats** something, add it to your notes.

Later, when you do your homework, go through your notes. Rewrite anything that is confusing or messy.✱ Make sure that you have written key words in the left-hand column. Add new key words to help you remember main ideas. Underline key words with colored pencils. Try grouping ideas by color.

You can also use this note-taking system when you're reading or studying on your own.

You can use a similar system if you are taking notes on a laptop or tablet. Ask your teacher for tips on what app to use and how to set it up.

Light	
transparent	can pass through
translucent	some can pass th...
opaque	cannot pass thro...

✱If there's something in your notes that's a total mystery, ask your teacher about it the next school day. Don't assume you'll figure it out when you need to—like the night before the test.

Two note-taking tips:

- **Skip lines between ideas.** That way, if you want to add more notes later to explain an idea, you'll have room.

- **Use only one side of the page.** Sometimes notes written on the backs of pages get "lost." You forget they're there.

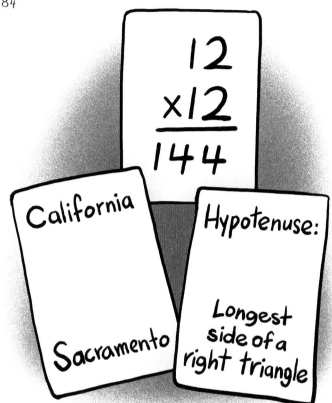

Simple Strategy 2
Use Note Cards and Flash Cards

Write key words and facts on note cards. Use flash cards to test your memory, especially in math and languages.

Tuck a few note cards and flash cards in your pocket or backpack. Peek at them during free moments (while waiting for the bus or waiting in line, for example).

Simple Strategy 3
Skim, Highlight, Read, Summarize

Before you start reading a passage, skim it. Flip through the pages and read just the topic sentences (first sentences) of each paragraph. Look at the pictures and read the captions. What do you think is the main idea?

If the book belongs to you, highlight the key words. If it doesn't, write the key words on note cards.

Next, read the passage carefully. It should be easier to understand because you've already skimmed it. Finally, summarize what you read by writing down a brief summary in your notebook or on your note cards.

Pssst!

Every week or so, check your desk, locker, backpack, homework place, and bedroom (including under your bed) for library books. Look at when they're due, and be sure to return them on time.

Library books are for everyone to use, so don't hog the ones you have. Keep them only as long as you need them. And take good care of them while you have them.

Take good care of all school property, including your desk, locker, tablet or laptop, and textbooks. These things don't belong to you. You're just using them until the next person comes along.

Memory Tips and Tricks

Try these ideas for remembering things you need to know for quizzes, tests, or just because.

Turn a list of words into an acronym. An acronym uses the first letter of each word to make a new word. **Examples:** NBA is the acronym for National Basketball Association. SCUBA is the acronym for Self-Contained Underwater Breathing Apparatus.

PEMDAS could be your acronym for remembering the order of operations in math: Parentheses, Exponents, Multiplication, Division, Addition, Subtraction.

Turn a list of words into a silly sentence. Do you need to remember the names of the planets in their order from the sun—Mercury, Venus, Earth, Mars, Jupiter, Saturn, Uranus, Neptune? Make up a sentence using the first letters of each planet's name: "My Very Educated Mother Just Served Us Nachos."

For the organization of living things (kingdom, phylum, class, order, family, genus, species), try: King Philip Came Over For Great Spaghetti.

Put a marble in your shoe. Do you have trouble remembering to bring your gym clothes to school on Tuesdays and Thursdays? Or do you forget your house key on Mondays and Fridays when you have to let yourself in to your apartment after school? Sometimes it's hard to remember things that don't happen every day or only happen once in a while.

Here's a way to remember occasional events. The night before, put a marble (or a stone, or something else small but hard) in your shoe. When you slip your foot into your shoe, you'll feel it, and your brain will go "AHA! There's something I need to remember!"

Talk it out. Say out loud what you're trying to learn. Instead of just seeing (reading), you'll also be **hearing** the sound of your voice and **feeling** your mouth make the words. The more senses you use while learning, the easier it is to remember what you learn.

Make up rhymes and songs. You probably learned the alphabet by singing the letters to the tune of "Twinkle, Twinkle, Little Star." Rhythm, repetition, rhyme, and melody can all help you remember things. "I before E except after C . . . " "Thirty days hath September . . . "

Chunk. It's hard to remember passwords as long strings: 2@255&3<82. It's much easier to remember them if you group the symbols and numbers into smaller chunks: 2@2 – 55&3 – <82. Chunking is one way to remember any long string of information, from a shopping list to historical dates.

Relate. Make a creative connection between old information and new information. **Example:** You already know that there's a country named Italy. Now you need to remember the name of an island close to that country— Sardinia. Imagine sardines on an Italian pizza.

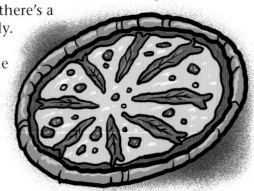

Plan to Stay Organized Day by Day

Each morning, look at your planner. Are you ready for the day?

Before you leave home for school, make sure you have everything you need for the day. Backpack? Binder? Tablet? Homework? Signed notes? Lunch? Special projects? What else?

At school, write your assignments on your homework checklist. Write due dates, quiz dates, and test dates in your planner.

Before you leave school for home, make sure you have everything you need for that night's homework. Handouts? Books? Worksheets? Notes? What else?

At home, stick to your homework schedule as closely as you can. Life happens, but try not to get off track too much.

Each night before you go to bed, look at your planner. Are you ready for tomorrow?

Each night before you go to bed, gather up everything you need for school the next day. Put it all in one place—on your desk, by the back door, or on the kitchen table. Try to use the same place every night.

Is It Worth It to Get Organized?

Maybe you're thinking, "Is it worth it to clean out my desk and locker and backpack and binder? Do I have to use a planner and fill out forms? Won't all that take a lot of time and effort?"

Sure it will—at first. But once you form the habit of being organized, it will take a lot **less** time and effort. And pretty soon you'll wonder why your desk was once a disaster, your locker was ever a shocker, and your backpack used to be a black hole.

For one thing, **your teacher** will notice your efforts to get organized. Teachers appreciate tidy desks and neat work turned in on time. That can help bring up your grades.

CLAP
CLAP
CLAP

Other kids at school will notice, too. They might compliment you for not being such a pigpen anymore. They might even ask you for pointers.

Your family will be grateful for the new, improved you. Who knows, some of your school habits could follow you home. Maybe you'll even start cleaning your room!

But most of all, you'll feel better about **yourself**. And you may have more free time than you ever imagined.

Experts say that disorganized people lose **one to two hours every day** looking for things, dealing with clutter, and procrastinating.

One to two hours every day times seven days a week equals seven to fourteen hours **every week.** That adds up to hundreds of hours every year.

Q: What will you do with that much extra time?

A: Whatever you want!

A Note for Parents and Teachers

Today's school environment is highly competitive. Kids who can't find their homework, their planner, or a decent pencil may suffer from poor grades and find school life more difficult.

No parent wants a child to fail a test just because he forgot to write it down in his planner. No teacher wants to give a student a lower grade just because she forgot her homework.

And anxiety is a real and serious issue for kids who lack organizational skills. When a student is unprepared and falls behind in her grades as a result, she can feel she's not up to the challenge. Over time, these small failures add up to stress inducers. Stress can lead to anxiety, and anxiety can impact school performance and even general happiness. Simply by being prepared, a student can feel more in control and less anxious.

If you're a parent, here's how to help your child become more organized:

- Begin slowly. Focus on one problem at a time.

- Start with "stuff management." Filing papers properly and neatly arranging study tools on a desk can be done fairly quickly. The results are concrete and motivating.

- Shop for supplies with your child. Guide his choices. Find supplies that match his needs, the school's guidelines, and your pocketbook.

- Make sure that your child has a proper study space at home—one that's quiet, brightly lit, and prepared with tools and storage boxes.

- Work with your child to determine the best time to study. Study time should be roughly the same time each weekday.

- Make sure that your child studies or reads even when she has no assigned homework.

- See to it that your child has a proper backpack. Help him clean out his backpack each evening. Make sure that he reloads it, so it's ready for school at the end of study time.

- Spend time looking through your child's planner with her. Show her how to use it. Check it each evening until she begins to use it consistently.

- Help your child manage electronics. No videos, apps, or texting during homework time. If your child has an electronic calendar, encourage him to use it and to set alerts to remind him of important events and due dates. Include the dates on a family calendar. Help your child organize his work on a tablet or laptop.

- Talk with your child's teacher. Get to know each other. A friendly, collaborative relationship will pay off handsomely for your child.

- Model organized behavior at home. Could you use some help? See page 101.

If you're a teacher, try these ideas:

- Schedule a weekly classroom cleanup time. Encourage students to organize their desks and lockers, and have them file, throw away, or take home loose papers.

- Permit responsible students to take home extra copies of heavy textbooks, if extras are available, or provide a classroom set or digital alternative.

- Teach a lesson on planner use early in the school year. Help students fill in planners daily. Check planners at the end of each day until students get the hang of them.

- Teach a lesson on accessing classroom materials on the school or class website. If you want students to turn in work electronically, make sure everyone understands how to do it.

- If your students use homework folders, make sure they put homework in their folders instead of cramming it into their backpacks or desks.

- Provide interim deadlines for long-term projects. Even older students budget time poorly until they gain experience.
- Model organized behavior. Keep your desk tidy and your papers filed.
- Talk with the parents of kids who seem especially disorganized. It's possible that parents and other family adults are not modeling organized behavior at home. Lots of adults have problems with organization! You might refer parents to some of the helpful resources described on page 101.

There's a fine line between helping kids get organized and doing it for them. The first teaches a life skill; the second reinforces dependency. With this in mind, both parents and teachers should:

- Keep expectations age-appropriate.
- Model appropriate choices, then allow independence.
- Permit kids to make mistakes without punishment. Reinforce that mistakes are learning opportunities.
- Allow for plenty of active fun time. Physical exercise is especially important for kids who tend to be disorganized.

Finally: Remember not to "lose it" yourself. Kids need to be kids, too! Which means that they will sometimes be messy, late, and disorganized. Try to be patient and don't expect perfection.

A few kids are born with a knack for organization. My own son wasn't one of them. It didn't happen overnight, but the strategies and techniques I taught him (and present in this book) have paid off. Now he's a happy, independent, self-confident young adult. What more could we parents and teachers ask for?

Helpful Resources

For Kids

B.J. Pinchbeck's Homework Helper
www.bjpinchbeck.com
Find hundreds of links to homework help. More than 10,000 people visit this site each day.

Fact Monster
www.factmonster.com
An award-winning site packed with reference materials, homework help, fun facts, and cool stuff.

Organizing from the Inside Out for Teens: The Foolproof System for Organizing Your Room, Your Time, and Your Life by Julie Morgenstern with Jessi Morgenstern-Colón (New York: Henry Holt and Company, 2002). Julie wrote a best-selling book for grown-ups on getting organized. Here she teams up with her daughter, Jessi, to help busy teens make the most of their space and time.

School Power: Study Skill Strategies for Succeeding in School by Jeanne Shay Schumm, Ph.D. (Minneapolis: Free Spirit Publishing, 2001). This book has strategies, charts, and checklists to help you read faster, study smarter, manage your time, track assignments, do better on tests, and more. Out of print, but it's a great resource that's available used and in libraries.

The 7 Habits of Highly Effective Teens by Sean Covey (New York: Touchstone, 2014). A best-selling guide for teens to build life skills and help them navigate life.

The Secrets of Top Students: Tips, Tools, and Techniques for Acing High School and College by Stefanie Weisman (Naperville, IL: Sourcebooks, 2013). Study strategies for teens that work, presented in a conversational manner.

Where's My Stuff? The Ultimate Teen Organizing Guide by Samantha Moss with Lesley Schwartz (San Francisco: Zest Books, 2010). Comprehensive advice for teens on organizing everything in their complicated lives.

For Parents and Teachers

Homework Without Tears: A Parent's Guide for Motivating Children to Do Homework and to Succeed in School by Lee Canter and Lee Hausner, Ph.D. (New York: William Morrow, 1987). This classic handbook helps parents deal with homework issues.

A Mind at a Time: America's Top Learning Expert Shows How Every Child Can Succeed by Mel Levine, M.D. (New York: Simon & Schuster, 2002). Children have unique learning styles, and this book helps parents and teachers identify appropriate ways to teach children as individuals.

Organizing from the Inside Out: The Foolproof System for Organizing Your Home, Your Office, and Your Life by Julie Morgenstern (New York: Henry Holt and Company, 2004). This *New York Times* bestseller has helped hundreds of thousands of people clean up the clutter in their lives.

SOAR Study Skills: A Simple and Efficient System for Earning Better Grades in Less Time by Susan Kruger (Lake Orion, MI: Grand Lighthouse Publishers, 2016). A best-selling guide on learning how to learn.

Study Is Hard Work: The Most Accessible and Lucid Text Available on Acquiring and Keeping Study Skills Through a Lifetime by William H. Armstrong (Jaffrey, NH: David R. Godine, 1995). This still-in-print classic by the author of *Sounder* offers a common-sense approach to learning that adults and older students will find invaluable.

Index

About the Author and Illustrator

Janet S. Fox is an author, mom, outdoor enthusiast, and former teacher. She's been to the bottom of the ocean in a submersible and had a brief fling with rock stardom. Her books are for children and young adults but have won her fans of all ages. Her newest novel, *The Charmed Children of Rookskill Castle*, is a gothic, middle grade fairy tale set in Scotland and has received starred reviews from *Kirkus*, *Publishers Weekly*, *Booklist*, and *Shelf Awareness*. She received an MFA in writing for children and young adults from Vermont College of Fine Arts in 2010, and at the moment, she's sporting blue stripes in her hair. She, her hubby, and their energetic dog live in Bozeman, Montana, where they enjoy the mountain vistas. Find out more at www.janetsfox.com.

Steve Mark is a freelance illustrator and a part-time puppeteer. He lives in Minnesota and is the father of three and the husband of one. Steve has illustrated several books in the Laugh & Learn series, including *Don't Behave Like You Live in a Cave* and *Bullying Is a Pain in the Brain*.

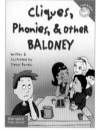